ENTREPRENEURSHIP

Dharma

Gita-Inspired Insights

ASISH DASH

Entrepreneurship
And

Dharma

Table of Contents

Entrepreneurship

And

Dharma

To Mom and Dad,

Thank you for always being there for me and loving me unconditionally.

Dad, your impatience and competitive nature taught me the importance of hard work and perseverance. Even though it was sometimes tough, your constant comparisons with others motivated me to strive for excellence.

I could not have accomplished all that I have without your love and support. You have always been my rock, my inspiration, and my biggest cheerleaders. Thank you for believing in me even when I doubted myself.

And to my loving wife,

Thank you for putting up with my endless work hours, my obsession with startups, and my never-ending desire to innovate. Your sarcasm and humor have been my constant source of laughter and joy, and I appreciate your patience and understanding more than words can express.

With love and gratitude,

Asish

Page intentionally left blank

Preface

Dear curious reader,

I invite you to join me on a journey that might seem unexpected at first, but trust me, it's worth it. In this book, we will explore the intersection between Bhagavad Gita and entrepreneurship - two seemingly unrelated subjects that have more in common than you might think.

As someone who has experienced success in the business world, I have come to realize that the teachings of the Bhagavad Gita can be incredibly valuable in navigating the complex and unpredictable landscape of entrepreneurship.

No,

We won't be chanting mantras or performing elaborate rituals before a board meeting (although if that's your thing, go for it!). Instead, we will delve into the principles of self-awareness, detachment, and focus on action rather than results that the Bhagavad Gita has to offer. Through the lens of entrepreneurship, we will examine how these principles can be applied in the pursuit of success and fulfillment.

But don't worry, this book won't be your typical dry and dull business read.

Instead, we will explore the timeless wisdom of the Bhagavad Gita in a lively and engaging manner, with plenty of anecdotes and humor sprinkled throughout.

So, whether you're an entrepreneur looking for a fresh perspective or just someone curious about the intersection of ancient wisdom and modern-day business, this book is for you.
So sit back, relax, and let's embark on this journey together.

Page intentionally left blank

Introduction

Have you ever found yourself pondering the meaning of success? Wondering if there's more to life than just the endless pursuit of material wealth and possessions?

If so, you're not alone.

As entrepreneurs, we are often driven by a desire for achievement and recognition, but we also crave something deeper - a sense of purpose and fulfillment.

That's where the Bhagavad Gita comes in.

This ancient Indian scripture offers profound insights into the nature of the self, the purpose of life, and the pursuit of happiness. And as it turns out, these insights are just as relevant to the world of entrepreneurship as they were thousands of years ago.

In this book, we will explore the intersection of Bhagavad Gita and entrepreneurship, and how the teachings of Vedic philosophy can help us navigate the complex and unpredictable landscape of modern-day business.

But before we dive in, let's take a closer look at what the Bhagavad Gita has to offer.

At its core, the Bhagavad Gita is a conversation between Arjuna, a warrior prince, and his charioteer Lord Shri Krishna, who is actually an incarnation of the divine.

Arjuna is faced with a dilemma - he must fight a battle against his own kinsmen, but he is hesitant to do so.

Krishna teaches him the principles of karma yoga, or the yoga of action, which emphasizes the importance of doing one's duty without attachment to the results.

This principle is especially relevant to entrepreneurship, where success is often measured by outcomes such as revenue, profit, and market share. But as Krishna teaches Arjuna, focusing too much on these outcomes can lead to anxiety and disappointment.

Instead, we must focus on doing our best and letting go of attachment to the results.

Another key principle of the Bhagavad Gita is the idea of dharma, or one's duty in life.

For Arjuna, his duty is to fight the battle and uphold his honor as a warrior.

But for entrepreneurs, our duty may be different - it may be to create products and services that improve people's lives, or to provide meaningful employment opportunities for our employees.

Ultimately, the Bhagavad Gita reminds us that success is not just about achieving our goals, but also about living a life of purpose and meaning.

It teaches us to cultivate self-awareness, to let go of attachment, and to focus on doing our duty with integrity and compassion.

So, if you're an entrepreneur looking for a new perspective on success, or simply someone curious about the wisdom of Vedic philosophy, this book is for you.

Together, we will explore the timeless teachings of the Bhagavad Gita and how they can be applied in the context of entrepreneurship.

But don't worry - this won't be a dry and academic read.

We'll explore these ideas in a fun and engaging way, with plenty of real-life examples and practical advice.

So, buckle up and get ready for a journey that will challenge your assumptions, broaden your horizons, and perhaps even change the way you think about success and happiness.

1. Delivering Results

कर्मण्येवाधिकारस्ते मा फलेषु कदाचन |
मा कर्मफलहेतुर्भूर्मा ते सङ्गोऽस्त्वकर्मणि || Bhagavad Gita 2.47

karmaṇy-evādhikāras te mā phaleṣhu kadāchana
mā karma-phala-hetur bhūr mā te saṅgo 'stvakarmaṇi

Here Lord Krishna tells us how we can practice karma Yoga. Karma Yoga means living in accordance with Karma - the natural laws that govern the universe. By understanding these laws and practicing acting according to them, one can gradually grow in wisdom and understanding.

Karma Yoga is a way to perform your duties diligently, but at the same time - it asks us to not get attached to the end results. Don't get upset when things don't go as planned.

Most people think they have a right to the rewards of their work, even if they haven't done any remarkable contribution.

Gita teaches us the opposite: you have a right to do your duty, but not expect the fruits of that action to come your way. Work is performed for spiritual gain, not just for physical reward. The purpose of any action is to grow in wisdom and knowledge.

The question is now: How can work result in a spiritual outcome?

Depending on the kind of work being done, whether it's being carried out properly or not in conformance to scripture or with materialistic standards of what is right and wrong, you will continue to operate at a level that is normally associated with the peers in your community/organization.

However, if you understand spiritual knowledge and make an effort to put it into practice, you will understand that you are a tiny soul and by following the path of Karma - you elevate the status of your soul - which can be done by attaining a higher level of spiritual intellect.

This is what has been termed by saints as: purifying oneself.

For example, the goal of studying is to learn, and the result is performance on an exam, thus studying not only helps us understand the material, but it also expands our minds. Through studying, a person increases their ability for thinking, reasoning, and grasping in addition to their understanding of the subject, and as a result, they improve their grades.

Similar to this, we carry out our responsibilities in this world with a spiritual perspective of life, which enables us to deepen our inner understanding and increase our knowledge. We become more aware of the fact that we are a soul and not a body when we act detachedly.

Goal of work is to grow in wisdom and not only acquire fruit.

A person's knowledge deepens more when they act on it. However, every task is carried out with a specific goal in mind. Hence, "mā phaleṣ hu kadāchana" does not imply that one shouldn't care at all about the outcome. The end result is what drives us, and it's okay if we want a certain outcome. The idea is to fulfill our obligations. and gain enlightenment.

It is more so important in business – be it startup or an organized MNC!

Most of the times founder's or top executives face this Self-Success bias where they may say that I have brought value to this project/company and so I am the sole cause of the success. They sometimes go on to re-affirm in their mind that the desired result would not have been achieved if they were not there and somebody else could simply not deliver results.

They believe they are the karma[1]–phala[2]-hetur.

For them *Krishna* has a very deep message, where He is saying ma[3] karma[4]–phala[5]-hetur bhur.

He is saying that one should not think that THEY are the ONLY reason for success, he guides us to work for the result – but also warns us that there are many other factors (which sometimes are beyond our control) to achieve success.

In a team there are always members who will believe in some superstitious things, which they believe are lucky for them, and will always do those stuff at the expense of acknowledging that they be termed "weird" or "foolish".

Surprisingly, they aren't either - nor foolish or weird.

Rather they understand that, there are things that are beyond our control which affects our results – which we term as destiny, fate or luck. When we are aware of the importance of such factors, we try to align ourselves with them and act accordingly.

---

1. http://vedabase.net/k/karma

2. http://vedabase.net/p/phala

3. http://vedabase.net/m/ma

4. http://vedabase.net/k/karma

5. http://vedabase.net/p/phala

I for instance – always prefer adorning the color black or shades of black for all my work-wear. Some term it superstitious, but for me it hides my cluttered work schedule.

I have the ability to hop multiple flights or roaming around the town jumping from one meeting to another, without bothering about creases, spots of sweat or dirt or getting worried about that drop of mayo accidentally falling from your burger. A dash of wipe with water is all it takes me to get ready for the next gig.

That's flexibility for me and that has worked so well for me till now, that the de-facto color for me while refreshing my wardrobe has been black all along – even subconsciously.

Gita teaches us to detach ourselves from the success of the result. Krishna suggests two levels of detachments, which are:

(i) Not to work for the sake of the result

and

(ii) while working not to attribute yourself as the reason for the result.

Now it's easier said than done, so here are a few ways you can work on detaching from success in your professional life:

> a) Focus on the process: Celebrate small wins and milestones along the way. This will keep the zeal high for you and your team, and help you focus better on the work to achieve final success. And if it were me, I also celebrate losses – to remind oneself that tomorrow is gonna be another great day and it's time to let go.
>
> *So cheer up and get your ass moving coz tomorrow I will win for sure!!!*

b) Set realistic goals: Setting unrealistic goals can create unnecessary stress and pressure. Make sure your goals are achievable and aligned with your values and priorities.

Unrealistic goals will only lead to burnout and affect the mental health of yours and anyone associated with you.

So let's keep it real and simple silly!

c) Embrace failure: Failure is part of the journey towards success. Rather than being discouraged by failures, use them as opportunities to learn and grow.

As I had discussed in my earlier books, a lot of entrepreneurs including me have witnessed setbacks in earlier life and now to think of it, I wouldn't have been here – if it weren't for the failures. They helped in the evolution of my mindset and that grit – which gives me confidence today, that no matter what – there is always a way out of all problems and I shall find them!

d) Practice gratitude: Be grateful for what you have already accomplished rather than constantly striving for more. This will help you appreciate the present moment and find fulfillment in the journey.

Don't be that person for whom, No success, No money is ever sufficient and in the process they start taking shortcuts and unethical business practices>

Dharma or no dharma, these shortcuts will accumulate and cost dearly one day!

e) Engage in non-work-related activities: Pursue hobbies and interests outside of work that bring you joy and happiness. This will help you maintain a healthy work-life balance and prevent your entire sense of self-worth from being tied to your professional success.

So now you know the Law of Karma, right!
It's not just some spiritual thing; it can totally be applied to business too!
For instance, say you're a startup founder trying to raise money for your biz.
You obviously gotta pitch to investors, but don't get too hung up on whether or not you get the funding. Just focus on making your pitch as awesome as possible, and let the investors decide.
Another example is a business owner launching a new product.
Of course, they need to get the word out and reach as many customers as possible, but don't obsess over hitting a certain number of sales. Instead, just focus on making the best possible product and promoting it in an ethical and effective way.
◇ The key here is to focus on doing what's right, rather than being solely obsessed with the outcome. By doing this, entrepreneurs can keep from getting too down when things don't go their way, and instead cultivate a sense of detachment and resilience that's vital for long-term success.
But don't think that you can just ignore the bottom line completely. You still gotta keep track of your progress and adjust strategies as needed.

The Law of Karma just says that you should focus on doing the right thing, and trust that good things will come from it.

So, one way to put the Law of Karma into practice is to focus on creating value for your customers and society at large, instead of just chasing profits.

Make products that solve real problems and fulfill actual needs, and you'll feel a sense of purpose beyond just making money.

Another way is to make sure your biz practices are ethical and sustainable.

Treat your employees, customers, and the environment with respect and care, and you'll build a reputation that can help you achieve long-term success.

In the end, the Law of Karma can be a powerful tool for entrepreneurs and business owners.

By focusing on doing what's right, rather than just obsessing over the outcomes, they can cultivate resilience, detachment, and purpose, all while making the world a better place.

The Gita focuses it so much on delivering results, that combined with the verse 2.47, there is another verse that reflects upon the notion of working hard without botheration of result.

What Dharma Says

तस्मादसक्त: सततं कार्यं कर्म समाचर ।

असक्तो ह्याचरन्कर्म परमाप्नोति पूरुष: ‖ Bhagavad Gita 3.19‖

tasmād asaktaḥ satataṁ kāryaṁ karma samāchara
asakto hyācharan karma param āpnoti pūruṣaḥ

Translation : Without being attached to the fruits of activities, one should act as a matter of duty, if you one desires to attain the Supreme!!

This verse emphasizes the importance of focusing on one's duty or work without becoming attached to the outcome.

Often, we become overly concerned with how others perceive our actions or appearance, but this verse reminds us that our ultimate goal should be to act without being attached to the results or opinions of others.

As a business coach, I have had the pleasure of working with many senior managers and leaders who have gone on to become successful leaders in their industries.

◇ One of the most important lessons I teach my protégé's is the importance of focusing on their duties or work without becoming attached to the outcome.

This concept is particularly relevant in today's world, where social media and other forms of technology have made it easier than ever for us to become overly concerned with how others perceive our actions and appearance.

The tendency to overestimate the extent to which our actions and appearance are noticed by others, can have a significant impact on our decision-making and leadership abilities.

When we become too focused on how others perceive us,

we may be less likely to take risks or make difficult decisions,

or

pursue opportunities that could benefit our businesses.

Instead, it is vital for leaders to focus on their duties or work without becoming attached to the outcome.

This means setting clear goals, developing a plan of action, and taking steps to achieve those goals without becoming overly concerned with the opinions of others.

When we are able to detach ourselves from the outcome and focus on our duties, we are more likely to make decisions that are in the best interests of our businesses and our teams.

Now, let's understand with an example!

◈ Imagine a CEO who is under pressure to increase profits from shareholders.

If the CEO becomes too focused on pleasing the shareholders and catering to their short-term goals, they may make decisions that prioritize immediate profits over the long-term growth and sustainability of the company.

However, if the CEO is able to detach themselves from external pressures and focus on their duties as a leader, they may be more likely to make decisions that prioritize the long-term success of the company, even if it means making difficult or unpopular choices in the short-term.

And this is what successful CEO's have been doing throughout – search the social media or business mags and you will find it a plenty instances of CEO bashing – whereas he/she was focused on the long term vision and results.

◈ Another example of the importance of focusing on one's duties rather than external validation can be seen in the case of a manager who is leading a team that is working on an important project.

If the manager becomes too focused on how the project will reflect on their personal reputation or how their superiors will perceive their performance, they may overlook the importance of empowering and motivating their team to work collaboratively and achieve the best possible results.

By concentrating on their responsibilities as a manager and empowering their team to perform their best, the manager can create a positive and productive work environment that ultimately leads to success.

In short, the importance of focusing on one's duties and responsibilities, without becoming too attached to external validation or opinions, cannot be overstated.

In any industry or leadership position, leaders must remain focused on the long-term goals of their company or organization and not let external pressures distract them from their ultimate objectives.

By setting clear goals, developing a plan of action, and taking steps to achieve those goals without becoming overly concerned with the opinions of others, leaders can become more effective and make better decisions for the benefit of their teams and organizations.

2. *When Fear Is Not An Option*

What Dharma Says:

नेहाभिक्रमनाशोऽस्ति प्रत्यवायो न विद्यते ।

स्वल्पमप्यस्य धर्मस्य त्रायते महतो भयात् ॥ Bhagavad Gita 2.40॥

nehābhikrama-nāsho 'sti pratyavāyo na vidyate
svalpam apyasya dharmasya trāyate mahato bhayāt

This verse is spoken by Lord Krishna to Arjuna during their conversation on the battlefield of Kurukshetra.

In this verse, Lord Krishna is assuring Arjuna that, even if one is not able to fully achieve their goals in this lifetime, there is no wasted. This verse emphasizes the importance of perseverance and steady effort in the practice of yoga and dharma. Even a little progress on this path can have a powerful impact, and there is no wasted effort in the pursuit of spiritual realization.

Success is a journey, not a destination.

The road to success is often paved with obstacles and challenges that may seem insurmountable at first. However, if we stay focused and persevere through difficult times, success is inevitable. One of the most profound teachings of the Gita is that nothing is lost and no effort is wasted in the pursuit of our goals.

This is exemplified by the analogy of planting a seed in the soil. When we plant a seed, we must water the soil constantly to ensure that the seed is not destroyed. Similarly, in our own lives, we must constantly water the seeds of our dreams and goals through hard work and dedication.

The Gita teaches that success is often achieved by doing difficult tasks.

Just as a seed must be planted and tended to in order to grow, we must put in the effort and time required to achieve our goals. However, the Gita also assures us that our efforts will not be in vain. Every action we take towards our goals produces its own good results in proper measure and at the proper time. Even if we don't achieve our goals in the way we had originally intended, we will still gain valuable experience and knowledge that can be applied to future endeavors.

In essence, the Gita encourages us to stay the course and persevere through difficult times. Success may not come easily or quickly, but with dedication and hard work, we can achieve our goals.

Remember, nothing is lost and no effort is wasted.

Every action we take towards our goals brings us one step closer to success.

So keep planting those seeds and watering them with diligence and patience.

Your success is just around the corner.

Modern day business guru's use the above concept to leverage the "Paradox of Fear"!

Pretty closely related...

As one starts his/her journey to become successful entrepreneur or business leader, one needs to understand that *Fear* can be both helpful and harmful to you when it comes to taking risks in business.

On one hand, fear can be useful when it signals that something may be risky or dangerous for your business. It helps you avoid making bad decisions that could hurt your business or finances.

For example, if you're thinking of investing in something risky, fear may tell you to take a step back and think about the potential risks and rewards.

On the other hand, fear can also hold you back and stop you from taking necessary risks to reach your goals.

If you're always afraid of failing or being rejected, you may miss out on opportunities for growth and success.

To illustrate this point, let's look at two successful entrepreneurs.

◈ Sara Blakely, the founder of Spanx, experienced fear when she first pitched her idea, but she used it to refine her pitch and business strategy.

◈ Elon Musk, the CEO of Tesla and SpaceX, took on risky projects like developing electric cars and exploring space, but he acknowledged the potential risks and benefits of his decisions.

Even in my close acquaintances I have seen it work.

So a friend of mine, Harsha started a coffee shop in the buzzing business district. He was passionate about his business and had invested all his savings into it, that he earned from his job as a software techie.

However unfortunately, the business was failing.

Harsha was losing money every month, and he couldn't figure out what was going wrong.

This went on for over 20 months and this was post Covid – so can't say that Covid affected him!!

One day we planned to meet over a cuppa coffee, and I visited him at the coffee shop for a free cuppa coffee that I learned to make in his kitchen.

It was here that Harsha confided about his struggles and how he was afraid of losing everything he had worked for.

I patiently listened to him and told him that fear was but natural at this juncture and that it could be helpful or harmful, depending on how he used it.

I encouraged Harsha to examine his fear and see if it was helpful or not.

We talked about how fear could be a useful signal to avoid risky investments or partnerships, but it could also hold him back from taking necessary risks to grow his business.

Though I did not expect it – but Harsha took my advice to heart and began to analyze his fears.

He realized that he was afraid of trying new things and taking risks because he didn't want to fail. However, he also realized that his fear was keeping him from making the changes he needed to turn his business around.

During the course of next few weeks, we both sat together and made a plan to address the issues in his business.

He started by revamping his menu and improving the quality of his coffee.

He also invested in marketing and started offering promotions to attract new customers.

At first, Harsha was afraid that these changes might not work, but he remembered about fear being a friend or a foe.

He used his fear to motivate him to work harder and to make sure that he was making the right decisions for his business.

Surprisingly enough - Over time, Harsha's business started to improve.

His customers were happy with the changes he had made, and he started to attract new ones.

He even started to make a profit again.

Harsha realized that he had used his fear to his advantage, and it had helped him turn his failing business around.

So, remember that *fear can be both helpful and harmful to you in business.*

Use it to your advantage by recognizing when it's helping you and when it's not.

Don't be afraid to take risks and learn from your mistakes.

With determination, resilience, and a healthy relationship with fear, you can become a successful entrepreneur and business leader.

I believe that winning over fear requires a comprehensive approach that involves a series of steps.

Here is my 7 step-by-step blueprint that has me overcome the fear of failure while doing business and everyday life.

Hope it helps you too!!

◈ Asish's 7 step guide to winning over fear

Step 1: Admit that fear is a normal thing

Everyone is afraid of something.

For some it's public speaking, trying something new, or not living up to one's own expectations. The first step to winning over the fear is to acknowledge that it's a completely normal thing.

It's okay to be afraid.

The important thing is to not let it control you.

Step 2: Ask yourself what you're afraid of

Once you've accepted that you're feeling fear,

it's time to identify what specifically you're afraid of!!

Is it the fear of failure, rejection, or making mistakes?

Or maybe it's the fear of the unknown.

Whatever it is, try to be as specific as possible.

Understanding what's causing your fear will help you come up with strategies to overcome it.

Step 3: Challenge your fears

Now it's time to face your fears head-on!

One way to do this is to challenge yourself to think about the worst-case scenario.

For example, if you're afraid of public speaking, imagine yourself giving a speech and completely messing it up.

Then, ask yourself if it was really that bad.

Most likely, the answer will be *NO*!!

In fact, you might learn something from the experience and become a better public speaker as a result.

Step 4: Take baby steps

You don't have to tackle your fear all at once.

Instead, take baby steps.

Start by doing something that makes you a little bit uncomfortable, but is still manageable.

For example, if you're afraid of networking events, start by attending a small event with people you know. Then, gradually work your way up to larger events with new people.

Step 5: Practice mindfulness

Mindfulness can be a powerful tool for managing fear and anxiety.

It involves being present and aware of your thoughts and feelings, without judgment.

Try to take a few minutes each day to practice mindfulness through meditation, deep breathing, or yoga. This will help you stay calm and centered when you're feeling afraid.

Step 6: Get support

It's important to have a support system when you're trying to overcome fear.

Talk to friends, family members, or a therapist about your fears and how you're working to overcome them.

Surround yourself with positive and supportive people who will encourage you and help you stay motivated.

Step 7: Celebrate your progress

Finally, celebrate your progress!

Even small achievements should be recognized and celebrated.

Pat yourself on the back for stepping out of your comfort zone and facing your fears.

Celebrating your progress will help keep you motivated and moving forward.

By following these seven steps, you should be able to overcome your fear and achieve your goals.

Remember, it is a process, so be patient and persistent in your efforts !!!!

3. Feel Other's Pain

What Dharma Says:

|| Bhagavad Gita 6.32 ||

ātmaupamyena sarvatra samaṁ paśhyati yo 'rjuna
sukhaṁ vā yadi vā duḥkhaṁ sa yogī paramo mataḥ

Here Lord Krishna says that, for him the perfect yogi is one - Who treats all living beings equally and cares about the happiness and sadness of others as their own !!

I have learnt about this idea of "servant leadership" from a around which my management philosophy resolves, for becoming a good leader.

The leadership lesson the verse suggests that devotion or reverence towards a higher purpose or principle is important in achieving success. In a business context, this could mean having a strong sense of values and ethics that guide decision-making and actions, and inspiring employees to align with these values as well.

This can lead to a more motivated and engaged workforce, as well as increased trust and loyalty among customers and stakeholders.

Now the term Servant leadership, I quoted above is a fancy way of saying that a good leader puts their team's needs first. It's all about collaboration and empathy, instead of just bossing people around.

I know the word "servant" might sound kind of weird or even offensive to some, but it's not meant to be taken literally.

It's just another way of saying that a leader should prioritize their team's well-being and success.

The cool thing about servant leadership is that it's quite contrary to traditional top-down leadership approaches. Instead of being a control freak, a servant leader focuses on building relationships with their team members, listening to their ideas and concerns, and providing them with the support and guidance they need.

By doing this, a servant leader can create a positive work environment built on trust and mutual respect.

And who doesn't want to work in an awesome place like that!!

I have personally worked for a boss like that, who believed in the philosophy of "servant leadership." and understood that his role as a leader was not to boss people around but rather to serve them and empower them to achieve their goals.

So in my early years, while I was working with a leading auto company on designing and my immediate boss was Mr.G.

Mr.G, the perfect cool boss was approachable, results-driven, and highly skilled at building relationships. He enjoyed socializing with staff but maintained a professional demeanor.

Now he knew that happy employees were key to a successful organization, so he made it a priority to create a positive work culture. He encouraged open communication and collaboration within his team, consistently recognized and rewarded good work, and ensured that his employees had the resources they needed to succeed.

So one day, I went to him with an absurd idea for a new product line, a new line of SUV engines. Initially, Mr.G was skeptical, but he listened carefully to my proposal and realized that it had potential.

So instead of dismissing my idea, Mr.G conveyed my idea to management and gave me the resources and support needed to bring the concept to life.

With the management's guidance and encouragement, me and my team were able to successfully create the beta product, which was something no-one had achieved in the shortest timeframe. Mr.G saw firsthand how empowering his employees could lead to significant growth.

As a result of Mr.G's servant leadership style, all his team members often felt valued and respected, which resulted in high morale and lowest attrition rates during his tenure. His employees were willing to go above and beyond to help the company succeed because they knew that their contributions were appreciated and that their leader had their best interests at heart.

In the end, Mr.G's commitment to servant leadership paid off, resulting in a thriving and successful organization that was built on trust, collaboration, and respect and he was promoted to the Global Leadership team to take the mantle forward.

So that was my personal story.

Let's take a well-established corporate example of the famous servant leadership style adopted by Herb Kelleher, the founder of Southwest Airlines.

Herb was a total game-changer when it came to leadership, and I think there are some valuable lessons that we can learn from him.

First off, Herb was all about putting others first.

He believed that leaders should serve their employees, customers, and communities, rather than using their power to control them.

As a CEO, it's important to remember that leadership is not about being a boss, but about being a servant. By focusing on the needs of others, you can create a more engaged and motivated workforce, and build a company that is truly customer-centric.

Herb was also a big believer in creating a positive and fun-loving culture.

He believed that a company's culture was essential to its success, and that leaders had a responsibility to create an environment that fostered creativity, innovation, and a sense of community.

As a leader, it's important to recognize that culture is not something that can be mandated or enforced; it's something that needs to be nurtured and cultivated over time.

By creating a supportive and empowering culture, you can attract and retain top talent and inspire your employees to give their best every day.

One of Herb's most significant contributions to the airline industry was his emphasis on customer service.

He believed that the key to success in business was to create a culture of service and to focus on delivering value to customers.

This meant not only meeting their needs but going above and beyond to exceed their expectations. It's crucial to remember that customers are the lifeblood of any business, and a customer-centric approach can make all the difference in creating a loyal customer base and achieving long-term success.

So, we have understood what servant-leadership style is – from my personal experience and from a well-established example.

Now comes the question, how do we incorporate it in practice.

So here it is :

Sr No.	Pointer	Description	Example
1	Put others first	Commitment to serving others by putting their needs first	Prioritizing employee development over personal career growth
2	Foster open communication	Encouraging open communication to better understand employee needs and perspectives	Implementing regular one-on-one meetings with employees to gather feedback
3	Build a positive culture	Creating a supportive and empowering environment for employees	Recognizing and celebrating employee accomplishments and milestones
4	Emphasize customer service	Prioritizing exceptional customer service by creating a culture of service	Providing personalized solutions to customer problems
5	Lead with humility	Showing humility and empathy in leadership	Acknowledging and learning from mistakes and failures

By adopting a servant leadership style, one can build a more engaged and motivated workforce, create a more positive and supportive culture, and deliver exceptional value to your customers.

Additionally, these organizations may also achieve higher levels of customer satisfaction and profitability due to the focus on employee well-being and empowerment.

In summary, my management philosophy for becoming a good leader is centered around servant leadership. By prioritizing the well-being of employees and empowering them to achieve their goals, leaders can foster a positive corporate culture and achieve long-term success for their organizations.

So, start today by putting these principles into practice and see the positive impact they can have on your organization!

4. Confirmation Bias

Confirmation bias is a psychological phenomenon where people tend to seek out information that confirms their pre-existing beliefs, while ignoring information that contradicts those beliefs. This can lead to narrow-minded thinking and an inability to consider alternative perspectives, ultimately hindering personal and professional growth.

This affects individuals across all sectors and professions, including business and entrepreneurship.

In the context of business and entrepreneurship, I often teach CXO's about the dangers of confirmation bias and its impact on decision-making. How it can lead to poor decision-making, a also result in lack of innovation, or create inability in adapting to changing circumstances.

For example, a business owner who is convinced that their product is the best on the market may ignore feedback from customers or fail to explore new technologies or trends. This can ultimately lead to a decline in business performance and competitiveness.

Now, the concept of confirmation bias is not explicitly discussed in the Bhagavad Gita. However, there are certain verses in the text that touch upon related themes.

What Dharma Says:

श्रीभगवानुवाच |

अशोच्यानन्वशोचस्त्वं प्रज्ञावादांश्च भाषसे |

गतासूनगतासूंश्च नानुशोचन्ति पण्डिता: || Bhagavad Gita 2.11 ||

śhrī bhagavān uvācha
aśhochyān-anvaśhochas-tvaṁ prajñā-vādānśh cha bhāṣhase
gatāsūn-agatāsūnśh-cha nānuśhochanti paṇḍitāḥ

Here Lord Krishna states that, "You mourn for those who should not be mourned for, yet you speak wise words. The wise grieve neither for the living nor for the dead."

This verse highlights the importance of critically evaluating our beliefs and perceptions, rather than blindly accepting them. It encourages us to approach situations with an open mind and consider multiple perspectives before drawing conclusions.

In business, making important decisions can have a significant impact on your company's success.

However, sometimes we might unconsciously interpret information to support our existing beliefs or opinions, while ignoring other facts that might contradict them.

This can lead to making bad decisions or missing out on opportunities that could have otherwise helped us grow and succeed.

For example, let's *take the case of Kodak.*

They were a successful company that had been in the film camera business for decades. However, they failed to embrace the emerging digital camera technology that was quickly taking over the market.

They were so attached to their traditional film-based camera model that they missed out on the opportunity to become a major player in the digital camera market, ultimately leading to their downfall.

◈ To avoid these kinds of mistakes, it's essential to cultivate a culture of critical thinking and open-mindedness within your organization.

Encouraging your team to question assumptions and consider multiple perspectives before making decisions can help ensure that you don't miss out on opportunities or overlook important facts.

For instance, you could have brainstorming sessions with your team, where everyone is encouraged to share their ideas and perspectives, regardless of their seniority or position.

Another example of the importance of critical thinking and open-mindedness can be seen in the success story of Amazon.

As we all know, Jeff Bezos started Amazon by selling books online.

However, he realized that there was an opportunity to expand into other products and services, such as music and video streaming, cloud computing, and even grocery delivery. By staying open to new ideas and being willing to take risks, Amazon has become one of the largest and most successful companies in the world.

To conclude, it's essential to approach decision-making with an open mind and consider multiple perspectives to avoid making bad decisions or missing out on opportunities.

Encouraging critical thinking and open-mindedness within your organization can help ensure that you stay on top of industry trends and are able to adapt to changing circumstances.

By doing so, you'll be better positioned to succeed in today's fast-changing business world.

Now the question that arises is, if there is some "set framework" to achieve the same!

Well, at Grazing Minds we happened to help a client do the same.

We helped them implement a culture of critical thinking and open-mindedness, and improved their decision-making processes. This helped to enhance their innovation and creativity, and ultimately helped them achieve greater success in today's complex and rapidly changing business environment.

What we adopted is a **'THINK'** framework, as follows:

T - Train and educate:

Invest in training and development programs for employees at all levels to facilitate critical thinking and decision-making. Focus on developing analytical skills, effective communication, and strategic thinking.

H - Harness diversity:

Foster a culture that values diversity and promotes the building of diverse teams with individuals from different backgrounds, perspectives, and experiences.

I - Invest in learning:

Encourage continuous learning and development to keep up with the rapidly changing business environment. Create a culture that values experimentation, promotes the acquisition of new skills and knowledge, and supports ongoing learning.

N - Nurture psychological safety:

Promote psychological safety within the organization to facilitate open communication, the sharing of ideas, and the challenging of assumptions. Create an environment where employees feel comfortable taking risks, speaking up, and providing feedback.

K - Keep evaluating and measuring:

Regularly evaluate and measure the effectiveness of the culture of critical thinking and open-mindedness. Use feedback mechanisms such as surveys, focus groups, or other methods to ensure that the organization is making progress towards its goals.

By following the Grazing Minds THINK framework, you too can develop a culture of critical thinking and open-mindedness in your organization that promotes innovation, creativity, and effective decision-making.

Another verse that addresses confirmation bias in the context of business and entrepreneurship is as:

What Dharma Says:

प्रवृत्तिंच निवृत्तिं च कार्याकार्य भयाभये |

बन्धं मोक्षं च या वेतिबुद्धिः सा पार्थ सात्त्विकी ||

|| Bhagavad Gita 18.30||

pravṛittiṁ cha nivṛittiṁ cha kāryākārye bhayābhaye

bandhaṁ mokṣhaṁ cha yā vetti buddhiḥ sā pārtha sāttvikī

Here Krishna Says that, the One who sees inaction in action, and action in inaction, is intelligent among men, and he is in the transcendental position, although engaged in all sorts of activities.

This verse challenges business owners and entrepreneurs to question their assumptions and look beyond the surface level of things. It reminds us that our perception of reality is often limited by our own biases and that we must strive to expand our understanding of the world.

As a business enthusiast, I interpret this verse as emphasizing the importance of knowledge, skill, and expertise in achieving success in business and entrepreneurship.

This verse underscores the significance of understanding the intricacies of business operations and developing specialized skills to effectively manage those operations. It also highlights the importance of knowledge-based decision making and the ability to analyze complex situations and make informed judgments.

For entrepreneurs, this shloka emphasizes the need for extensive knowledge and expertise in their field of business.

Successful entrepreneurship requires not only a good idea but also a deep understanding of the industry, market trends, customer behavior, and other critical factors that impact the success of a business venture.

Now let's drill down more into it and understand with case studies and simple terms!

Let's say you want to start a business that sells eco-friendly cleaning products.

You have a passion for the environment and believe there is a growing demand for sustainable household products. However, simply having a good idea is not enough to ensure success.

To be successful, you need to have knowledge about the industry, including the market size, competition, and customer preferences.

You also need specific skills related to managing a business, such as accounting, marketing, and supply chain management. With this knowledge and skillset, you can develop a solid business plan that takes into account all of these factors and positions your product for success.

Additionally, you need to base your actions on knowledge alone. This means that you should be constantly learning and adapting your strategies based on new information and feedback from customers. By being open to new ideas and approaches, you can refine your business model and improve your chances of success.

Now let's consider a hypothesis:

Imagine two entrepreneurs who both have a passion for creating sustainable fashion.

◈ The first entrepreneur has extensive knowledge of the fashion industry, including trends, design techniques, and marketing strategies. They also have strong connections within the industry and have built a network of suppliers and retailers.

◈ The second entrepreneur has a great idea for a sustainable fashion line but lacks knowledge and experience in the fashion industry.

Based on our understanding of Chapter 18, verse 30 of Bhagavad Gita (above), we would predict that the first entrepreneur is more likely to achieve success than the second.

By leveraging their knowledge and skillset, the first entrepreneur is better equipped to navigate the complexities of the fashion industry and make informed decisions that maximize their chances of success.

The second entrepreneur, while passionate and well-intentioned, may struggle to overcome the knowledge gap and may face more setbacks and challenges as a result.

This serves as a reminder that true success in business and entrepreneurship comes not from blind action, but from a combination of knowledge, skill, and wise decision-making.

The Bhagavad Gita also stresses the importance of humility and a willingness to learn from others.

What Dharma Says:

तद्विद्धि प्रणिपातेन परिप्रश्नेन सेवया |

उपदेक्ष्यन्ति ते ज्ञानं ज्ञानिनस्तत्त्वदर्शिन: ||

||Bhagavad Gita 4.34||

tad viddhi praṇipātena paripraśhnena sevayā
upadekṣhyanti te jñānaṁ jñāninas tattva-darśhinaḥ

Here Shri Krishna says, Just try to learn the truth by approaching a spiritual master. Inquire from him submissively and render service unto him. The self-realized souls can impart knowledge unto you because they have seen the truth.

For me, this verse emphasizes the importance of seeking guidance and mentorship from experienced individuals who have already achieved success in their respective fields.

Just as a spiritual guru can guide a seeker on their path towards enlightenment, a business mentor can guide an entrepreneur towards success in their venture.

This highlights the importance of *approaching a mentor with humility and a willingness to learn.*

Now, let's understand how this plays out in the real world scenario.

Let's say you are an aspiring entrepreneur who wants to start a business, but you're not sure where to begin.

You might consider seeking out a mentor who has experience in your industry or field of interest. This mentor could be someone who has started their own successful business, or perhaps a seasoned executive with years of experience in your particular industry.

You might ask them for guidance on topics such as developing a business plan, attracting investors, or building a team.

The mentor, in turn, can impart knowledge and advice based on their own experiences and successes. They can offer insights on what has worked well for them, as well as cautionary tales of some mistakes they have made along the way.

◈ *They can save you time and money by helping you avoid common pitfalls and providing guidance on best practices.*

Now it's important to note here, that finding a mentor isn't always easy.

It takes effort and persistence to identify someone who is willing and able to provide guidance. But the benefits of a good mentor can be invaluable to an entrepreneur, particularly in the early stages of building a business.

Overall, this verse underscores the critical role that mentorship and guidance can play in the development of successful entrepreneurs and business leaders. By seeking out the right mentors and approaching them with humility and a willingness to learn, aspiring entrepreneurs can gain invaluable insights and support on their journey towards success.

5. The Power of Inaction

When we are faced with difficult decisions or challenging situations, our natural inclination is often to take action.

We feel a sense of urgency to do something, anything, in order to alleviate the problem or move toward a solution.

However, there are times when not acting can be the most powerful choice we can make.

I have discussed about the same in my earlier book series – "Insights from a shy entrepreneur" too, but here we understand it in a more Dharmic way and build our business around it's learning's.

⬦ *Inaction can sometimes be seen as weak or indecisive,*

but there is a growing research that suggests that there is great power in intentional inaction.

This concept challenges us to consider the potential benefits of restraint, patience, and reflection, and to recognize that sometimes the best action is no action at all.

What Dharma Says:

कर्मणो ह्यपि बोद्धव्यं बोद्धव्यं च विकर्मण: |

अकर्मणश्च बोद्धव्यं गहना कर्मणो गति: ||

||Bhagavad Gita: 4.17||

karmaṇo hyapi boddhavyaṁ boddhavyaṁ cha vikarmaṇaḥ
akarmaṇaśh cha boddhavyaṁ gahanā karmaṇo gatiḥ

Lord Krishna tells us that,

He who sees inaction in action and action in inaction, he is a wise man among men; he is a yogi and performer of all actions!!

This verse suggests that one should have a balanced perspective on action and inaction. Sometimes, taking no action can be just as important as taking action.

A truly wise person understands this balance and is able to make the best decisions based on their circumstances. While luck may play a role, it is ultimately up to the individual to act in a way that aligns with their goals and values.

◈ Modern B-schools and Business Guru's have borrowed upon this idea to define the term, ***_situational leadership_***, where the emphasis is on the importance of adapting one's actions to the specific situation - which Lord Krishna advised to Arjuna above!!

Situational leadership is a leadership theory that emphasizes the importance of adapting one's leadership style to the specific situation. According to situational leadership, effective leaders are those who are able to identify the needs and capabilities of their followers and adjust their leadership style accordingly.

Both situational leadership and the Bhagavad Gita verse recognize that there is no one-size-fits-all approach to leadership or decision-making.

Instead, effective leaders must be able to assess the situation and make decisions based on the needs and capabilities of those involved.

◈ In today's world, being an entrepreneur or leader means you need to be able to analyze your actions and their effects on your business.

This includes figuring out what worked well and what didn't, so you can make better choices in the future. There are also times when you absolutely have to take action in order to move forward and make progress.

So, it's important to be able to recognize when to act and when to hold back.

Ultimately, being a successful entrepreneur or leader isn't just about making decisions, it's about understanding when to make them and how they'll impact your business in both the short and long term..

So let's understand it better with some case-studies.

◈ Let's begin with today's Iconic company: Apple and it's founder!

Steve Jobs' leadership style is often studied and revered in the field of business management. One of the key aspects of his success was his ability to identify when inaction was the best course of action.

In the late 1990s, Apple was struggling and on the brink of bankruptcy.

Instead of panicking and making a rash decision, Jobs took a step back and reevaluated the company's strategy. He understood that Apple had been trying to do too many things at once and that they needed to focus on a few key products.

This decision to prioritize and streamline the company's offerings ultimately paid off, leading to the incredible success that Apple has achieved today.

By recognizing the importance of inaction and taking the time to carefully analyze the situation, Jobs was able to make a strategic decision that had a major impact on the company's trajectory. As a leader, it's important to emphasize the significance of not always feeling the need to take immediate action. Sometimes, taking a step back allows for a clearer perspective and can lead to better decision-making. The case of Steve Jobs and Apple serves as a great example of this principle in action.

◈ Another example of another great business leader of today's time – Elon Musk!

Everyone will agree that Musk is a prime example of a leader who has demonstrated strategic thinking in action.

As the CEO of three high-profile companies, Tesla, Twitter and SpaceX, he has faced numerous challenges and obstacles throughout his career. In particular, his approach to risk-taking and decision-making highlights several key elements of strategic thinking that have contributed to his success.

One notable example of Musk's strategic thinking was his decision to take a step back from the problem of developing a reusable rocket.This was a difficult challenge that many experts had deemed nearly impossible due to the complexity of the engineering required.

Rather than charging ahead and throwing resources at the problem, Musk recognized the need for a more thoughtful approach.

By taking a pause and focusing on other projects, Musk was able to preserve resources and avoid *the sunk cost fallacy* - the tendency for individuals and organizations to continue investing in a project even when it is unlikely to succeed.

This demonstrates Musk's ability to recognize the importance of prudence and calculated risk-taking, both of which are key elements of strategic thinking.

Moreover, Musk's decision to delay solving this problem until he was better prepared also reflects his recognition of the value of inaction.

While it can be tempting to always be busy and productive, sometimes the best course of action is to step back and reassess priorities. By doing so, Musk was able to achieve greater clarity on his goals and develop a more effective plan for tackling the reusable rocket challenge.

In the end, combining boldness with prudence, calculated risk-taking, and recognizing the value of inaction when necessary have all been essential components of Elon Musk's strategic thinking. These traits have allowed him to achieve impressive results, such as successfully launching reusable rockets and making groundbreaking advancements in electric vehicles, among others.

◇ Now we have understood with examples the importance of adapting one's actions to the specific situation. But how do we practice it in real life, happens to be the big question!?!?!?!

For day-to-day purposes we have the *"VIBGYOR"* frame-work, through which leaders can adapt their leadership style to the needs of the situation, and make better decisions that align with the principles outlined in Bhagavad Gita

Let's dig into the details.

◈ **"VIBGYOR"** which stands for:

V - Visualize the task at hand and the context of the situation

This step emphasizes the importance of understanding the task or goal at hand, as well as the broader context of the situation. Effective leaders should have a clear vision of what needs to be accomplished and how it fits into the bigger picture. They should also consider external factors that may impact the situation, such as market trends, competition, or regulatory changes.

I - Identify the needs and capabilities of the team members

This step involves assessing the skills and knowledge of the team members and identifying their individual strengths and weaknesses. Effective leaders should be able to match the right people to the right tasks, and provide the necessary support and guidance to help team members develop their skills.

B - Balance between positive and negative actions, and discern when inaction is the best course of action

This step is inspired by the above Bhagavad Gita verse 4.17, which emphasizes the importance of discerning when inaction is the best course of action. Effective leaders should be able to balance positive and negative actions, and know when to take action and when to refrain from action. This requires a deep understanding of the situation and the ability to make informed decisions based on available information.

G - Guide the team members by providing clear expectations and directions

This step involves communicating clear expectations and directions to the team members. Effective leaders should be able to articulate the goals and objectives of the task, as well as the specific roles and responsibilities of each team member. This helps to ensure that everyone is on the same page and understands what is expected of them.

Y - Yield to the situation by adapting the leadership style to the needs of the situation

This step emphasizes the importance of being flexible and adaptable in one's leadership style. Effective leaders should be able to adjust their approach to the situation, based on the needs and capabilities of the team members. This may involve using different leadership styles, such as directing, coaching, supporting, or delegating, depending on the needs of the situation.

O - Offer support and feedback to the team members to help them improve

This step involves providing ongoing support and feedback to the team members. Effective leaders should be able to identify areas where team members need assistance, and provide the necessary resources and guidance to help them improve. They should also provide regular feedback on performance, to help team members identify areas for improvement and continue to develop their skills.

R - Reflect on the outcome and adjust the approach as needed

This step emphasizes the importance of reflecting on the outcome of the task or project and making adjustments as needed. Effective leaders should be able to evaluate their own performance, as well as the performance of the team members, and make changes to the approach as necessary. This helps to ensure continuous improvement and enables the team to achieve better results over time.

In conclusion, the VIBGYOR blueprint is a great way for business leaders to implement situational leadership in their day-to-day activities.

So, give VIBGYOR a try and see how it can help you become a better leader!

6. Balance For Success

The Bhagavad Gita emphasizes the importance of balance and moderation in all aspects of life.

Often in many chapters, Lord Krishna teaches Arjuna that he should perform his duty without being attached to the results of his actions. The repetition is because, by finding a balance between effort and detachment, one can optimize their performance and achieve success.

Furthermore, the Bhagavad Gita teaches that one should not be swayed by emotions or desires, but should act with clarity and equanimity.

What Dharma Says:

नात्यश्नतस्तु योगोऽस्ति न चैकान्तमनश्नतः |

न चाति स्वप्नशीलस्य जाग्रतो नैव चार्जुन ||

||Bhagavad Gita: 6.16||

nātyaśhnatastu yogo 'sti na chaikāntam anaśhnataḥ
na chāti-svapna-śhīlasya jāgrato naiva chārjuna

This means "There is no possibility of one's becoming a yogi, O Arjuna, if one eats too much or eats too little, sleeps too much or does not sleep enough."

In this verse, Lord Krishna advises Arjuna that finding balance in all aspects of life, including eating and sleeping, is important for leading a balanced and fulfilling life.

This verse emphasizes the importance of balance and moderation in one's lifestyle to achieve spiritual progress and self-realization. The verse suggests that excessive indulgence or deprivation can hinder one's ability to focus and attain the desired goal.

Balance and moderation in various aspects of life are essential for optimal performance and success, whether it is in spiritual practice or business leadership.

◈ As leaders, it is crucial to recognize the impact of physical and mental health on our ability to perform and make sound decisions. A healthy work-life balance and self-care practices, such as proper nutrition and sufficient sleep, can lead to increased productivity, better decision-making, and sustained success in the long run.

Similarly, in entrepreneurship, excessive focus on work at the expense of personal well-being can lead to burnout and negatively impact the success of the venture. On the other hand, neglecting work and failing to prioritize business tasks can result in missed opportunities and stunted growth.

The above wisdom provided by Lord Krishna has been adapted by many philosophers and cultures. Let's understand some of them for a better over-view of the teaching.

> - One example is the Japanese concept of "Kaizen,"
>   which means continuous improvement.

This principle emphasizes the importance of making small, incremental changes over time to improve processes and systems in a balanced and sustainable way. This approach has been applied by many successful Japanese companies, such as Toyota, to achieve long-term success.

- Another example is the Indian concept of "Seva," which means selfless service.

This principle emphasizes the importance of balancing personal ambition with a sense of social responsibility and serving others. Many successful Indian entrepreneurs, such as Ratan Tata, have applied this principle to create businesses that not only generate profits but also serve the greater good.

- In the context of personal well-being, the practice of Yoga, originating from ancient India, emphasizes the importance of finding balance and moderation in one's physical, mental, and spiritual health.

This practice has gained worldwide popularity and has been shown to improve overall health and well-being.

- Finally, the Chinese philosophy of Yin and Yang emphasizes the importance of finding balance between opposing forces.

This principle has been applied in many aspects of business and leadership, such as balancing risk and reward, and balancing short-term and long-term goals.

In conclusion, the Asian sub-continent has provided many examples of how balance and moderation have been applied in business and leadership to achieve sustained success. These principles emphasize the importance of finding a balanced approach to achieve success in all aspects of life, including personal well-being, professional goals, and social responsibility.

Similarly, for the B-school students - the Yerkes-Dodson law proposes that there is an optimal level of arousal for a given task, and too little or too much arousal can negatively affect performance. According to the law, moderate levels of arousal lead to optimal performance, whereas low levels of arousal result in boredom and apathy, and high levels of arousal lead to anxiety and stress. From a personal perspective, the above verse has helped me unlock a lot of aspects in my life. For instance, balance and moderation helped me in achieving success in the following manner:

    i. ***Improved health*** - Finding a balance between work and personal well-being, practicing self-care, and maintaining a healthy lifestyle helped me improve my physical and mental health.
This lead to increased productivity, better decision-making, and sustained success in the long run.

    ii. ***Increased productivity*** - When we are well-rested, nourished, and in good health, we are more likely to be productive and efficient in our work. Additionally, finding the right balance of challenge and skill in our work can lead to increased motivation and engagement, resulting in higher productivity.

    iii. ***Better decision-making*** - When we are balanced and grounded, we are more likely to make sound decisions.

This is because balance and moderation help us to maintain clarity, focus, and a rational mindset, which are essential for effective decision-making.

iv. *Improved relationships* - Balance and moderation can also improve our relationships with others. When we are well-balanced, we are more likely to be empathetic, patient, and understanding, leading to improved communication and collaboration with others.

v. *Increased resilience* - Finding balance and moderation in our lives helps us to build resilience, enabling us to handle stress, challenges, and setbacks more effectively. This resilience allows us to bounce back quickly from setbacks, maintain a positive attitude, and remain focused on our goals.

In conclusion, finding balance and moderation in all aspects of life, including work, personal well-being, and relationships, is essential for achieving sustained success in management and leadership.

Now, one may say – everyone talks about the positives, what if I don't follow it?

What will be the consequences?

From my personal experience, let me explain some of the consequences of imbalance:

i. **Burnout** - One of the most common consequences of imbalance is burnout. This can occur when we spend too much time and energy on work, neglecting their personal well-being and other aspects of their life. Burnout can lead to exhaustion, cynicism, and a sense of ineffectiveness, which can have negative impacts on productivity and well-being.

ii. **Reduced productivity** - Imbalance can lead to reduced productivity, as we may struggle to focus, make sound decisions, and complete tasks efficiently. This can be due to stress, fatigue, and poor mental and physical health.

iii. **Poor decision-making** - When we are imbalanced, we struggle to make sound decisions. This can be due to factors such as stress, fatigue, and a lack of mental clarity. Poor decision-making can have negative impacts on business outcomes, relationships with colleagues, and personal well-being.

iv. **Strained relationships** - Imbalance can also lead to strained relationships with colleagues, friends, and family. This can occur when we are too focused on work or personal pursuits, neglecting our relationships and social connections. Strained relationships often lead to decreased morale, poor communication, and a negative work environment.

v. **Health problems** - Imbalance can lead to a range of health problems, such as chronic stress, sleep deprivation, and poor nutrition. These health problems have negative impacts on productivity, well-being, and long-term health outcomes.

To sum it up, imbalance can have a range of negative consequences in management and leadership. As a result, finding balance and moderation in all aspects of life is essential for achieving sustained success and well-being.

Now, my intention was not to make you conscious or make you fearful about maintaining balance in life.

Some may ask, ***how do we find balance?***

Well, there are several approaches to finding balance – let's discuss some here:

- Work-life balance:

This approach focuses on balancing work commitments with personal and family time. It involves prioritizing personal well-being, hobbies, and relationships alongside work responsibilities. Strategies for achieving work-life balance may include setting boundaries, delegating tasks, and taking time off.

- Mind-body balance:

This approach focuses on balancing physical health with mental and emotional well-being. It involves practices such as exercise, meditation, and mindfulness to reduce stress, improve focus, and promote overall well-being.

- Workload balance:

This approach focuses on balancing the volume and complexity of work tasks with an individual's capacity to complete them. It involves strategies such as prioritization, time management, and delegation to ensure that tasks are completed efficiently without causing undue stress.

- Values-based balance:

This approach focuses on balancing an individual's personal values and goals with their work commitments. It involves aligning personal values and goals with organizational goals to promote a sense of purpose and fulfillment in work.

- Social balance:

This approach focuses on balancing work relationships and social connections with work commitments. It involves nurturing positive relationships with colleagues and building social connections outside of work to promote a sense of community and support.

So there are several approaches to finding balance in life.

By prioritizing balance in all aspects of life, we can achieve sustained success and well-being in our personal and professional lives.

Now, these were theoretical tools.

Let me help you with ***some practical tools and resources*** that you can use to find balance and moderation in your lives:

1) Time management tools: Time management tools such as calendars, to-do lists, and time-tracking apps can help you prioritize your tasks and ensure that you are not overloading yourself with work.

This can help them balance their workload and prevent burnout.

2) Mindfulness and meditation apps: Mindfulness and meditation apps such as Headspace and Calm can help you reduce stress, improve focus, and pro-

mote mental well-being. These tools can be useful for achieving mind-body balance and reducing the negative effects of stress.

3) Self-care resources: Self-care resources such as self-help books, wellness websites, and fitness apps can help you prioritize your physical and mental health. These resources can provide guidance on topics such as nutrition, exercise, and stress management.

4) Support networks: Building support networks of friends, family, and colleagues can help you further achieve social balance and prevent feelings of isolation. These networks can provide emotional support and encourage students to prioritize their personal relationships.

5) Coaching and counseling services: Coaching and counseling services provided by professionals can provide you with personalized support and guidance on achieving balance and moderation in your lives. These services can help oneself identify areas where one may be imbalanced and provide strategies for achieving greater balance.

In short, there are several practical tools and resources that one can use to achieve balance and moderation in their lives.
As future leaders, we must prioritize self-care and strive to find balance in our work and personal lives to achieve sustained success and fulfillment.

7. Aligned Capabilities

We all know that the Bhagavad Gita has been transmitted and translated across different regions and cultures over time. It has influenced many aspects of Indian culture and philosophy, and has also been studied and commented upon by scholars around the world.

It has been translated into different languages and adapted to different cultural contexts. For example, the first English translation of the Bhagavad Gita was done by Charles Wilkins in 1785, and since then the text has been translated into many other languages, including German, French, Spanish, and Russian.

Each of these translations reflects the cultural background and linguistic style of the translator, and thus adds another layer to the multicultural tapestry of the text.

The Bhagavad Gita highlights the enduring relevance and universality of the text, which continues to inspire and influence people from all walks of life and as we come towards the end of this book – we need to understand the interconnectedness of different cultures and traditions throughout history, and how the transmission of ideas and knowledge has shaped our world.

This has been highlighted through various verses of the Gita, for instance in Chapter 6, Verse 32 (about which we discussed in Chapter 3 of this book), where Lord Krishna implies that all things are interconnected and ultimately linked to the divine, and that by recognizing this unity we can achieve a state of enlightenment

And

Chapter 4, Verse 11 – which states:

ये यथा मां प्रपद्यन्ते तांस्तथैव भजाम्यहम् |

मम वर्त्मानुवर्तन्ते मनुष्या: पार्थ सर्वश: || 4.11||

ye yathā māṁ prapadyante tāns tathaiva bhajāmyaham

mama vartmānuvartante manuṣhyāḥ pārtha sarvaśhaḥ

Where it is suggested that all paths lead to the divine, and that every individual's journey is unique and valid in its own right.

Overall, The Bhagavad Gita conveys a message of interconnectedness and unity that is consistent with this idea.

Till now, we have taken a particular teaching from the Gita and implemented a business study to incorporate in our day-to-day business life. But learning or functioning in singularity had never been the case. Each and every learning is always inter-related to look at the bigger picture.

Now let's take this further and understand the inter-aligned valuable teachings on leadership, strategy, and ethics that The Gita gives us:

i. Focus on core competencies:

In the Bhagavad Gita, Lord Krishna emphasizes the importance of focusing on one's dharma or duty. This means that individuals should focus on their inherent strengths and capabilities and use them to serve society.

श्रेयान्स्वधर्मो विगुण: परधर्मात्स्वनुष्ठितात् |

स्वधर्मे निधनं श्रेय: परधर्मो भयावह: ||3.35||

shreyān swa-dharmo viguṇaḥ para-dharmāt sv-anuṣhṭhitāt
swa-dharme nidhanaṁ shreyaḥ para-dharmo bhayāvahaḥ

This verse teaches the importance of following one's own duty or dharma, rather than trying to imitate the actions of others. The verse says, "It is better to perform one's own duty, even though imperfectly, than to perform someone else's duty perfectly."

This verse can be applied to the field of management as a lesson on the importance of focusing on one's core competencies.

As a business leader, it's essential to take a close look at what your company does best.

What are your unique strengths and abilities that set you apart from your competitors? For example, is your company particularly adept at providing exceptional customer service, or do you have a cutting-edge technology that no one else in the market has?

Once you've identified your core competencies, it's essential to focus on developing them even further. This may involve investing in additional training or resources to bolster your strengths.

For example, if your company is known for its excellent customer service, you may want to invest in additional training programs for your employees to enhance their communication and problem-solving skills.

Another key lesson that Chapter 3, Verse 35 of the Bhagavad Gita teaches is the importance of taking action, even if it's imperfect.

As a CEO, it's crucial to foster a culture of experimentation and encourage your team to take calculated risks. For example, you may want to launch a new product or service, even if it's not perfect yet, to gain valuable feedback from customers and make improvements.

In addition, it's important to avoid the temptation to imitate the strategies and tactics of your competitors. Instead, focus on your own strengths and develop strategies that align with your unique core competencies.

For example, if your company is known for its cutting-edge technology, you may want to invest in research and development to stay ahead of the curve, rather than copying the strategies of your competitors.

By following these lessons from the Bhagavad Gita and focusing on your core competencies, taking action, and avoiding imitation, you can position your company for long-term success in today's competitive business landscape.

i. Collaboration and partnerships:

The Bhagavad Gita teaches the importance of working together and building strong relationships. As Lord Krishna says in Chapter 9, Verse 22,

श्रेयान्स्वधर्मो विगुण: परधर्मात्स्वनुष्ठितात् |

स्वधर्मे निधनं श्रेय: परधर्मो भयावह: ||9.22||

shreyān swa-dharmo viguṇaḥ para-dharmāt sv-anuṣhṭhitāt
swa-dharme nidhanaṁ shreyaḥ para-dharmo bhayāvahaḥ

"I am the same to all beings; to Me there is none hateful or dear. But those who worship Me with devotion are in Me and I am in them."

Shri Krishna emphasizes the importance of exclusive devotion and meditation on the divine form of the ultimate reality. Those who worship with such devotion and focus will be granted what they lack and will have their needs taken care of.

This verse highlights the importance of trust and faith in one's partners.

Just as devotees have faith in the divine to provide for them, partners must trust each other to deliver on their commitments and take care of each other's needs. This requires a deep level of commitment and exclusive focus on the partnership, with both parties working towards a common goal.

The Gita also suggests that the divine carries what the devotees lack and preserves what they have.

Similarly, in a partnership, each partner should contribute their unique strengths and resources, while also being mindful of the other partner's needs and limitations. By doing so, they can work towards shared success and prosperity.

The above verse also emphasizes the importance of a selfless attitude towards partnerships.

By focusing on the needs of the partnership as a whole, rather than individual needs, partners can achieve a greater level of success and fulfillment. This requires an attitude of service towards the partnership and a willingness to work towards the greater good, rather than individual gain.

Let's dwell further with the basis of some examples and extrapolate some management lessons built on the above wisdom.

One of the classic example I am reminded of, is the collaboration in business between **Starbucks and PepsiCo.**

So, In 1994 both the companies formed a partnership to distribute Starbucks ready-to-drink coffee and tea products. This collaboration allowed Starbucks to expand its reach beyond its physical stores, and PepsiCo to enter the premium coffee and tea market.

This connects with the resource-based view (RBV) of management theory, which emphasizes the importance of a company's resources and capabilities in creating a sustainable competitive advantage.

By collaborating with PepsiCo, Starbucks was able to leverage the distribution and marketing capabilities of its partner, which allowed it to expand its product offering and reach new customers. This joint venture also allowed both companies to benefit from each other's strengths, resources, and capabilities, creating a mutually beneficial partnership.

Similar is a story of the partnership between **Nike and Apple.**

In 2006, Nike and Apple collaborated to create the Nike+ running system, which combined Nike's running shoes with Apple's iPod music player and sensor technology to track and monitor running performance.

This collaboration allowed Nike to enhance its product offering and differentiate itself from competitors, while Apple was able to leverage Nike's brand and expertise in the sports industry.

This example resonates with the strategic alliances management theory, which focuses on the formation and management of partnerships between firms to achieve strategic goals.

The Nike+ running system partnership allowed both companies to benefit from each other's expertise and capabilities, creating a product that was unique and differentiated from competitors. This partnership also allowed both companies to reach new customers and enhance their brand image, creating value for both partners.

The above two examples demonstrate how collaboration and partnerships can be effective strategies for businesses to achieve their goals and create value.

By leveraging each other's resources and capabilities, companies can gain a competitive advantage, expand their reach, and create mutually beneficial partnerships. These also connect with management theories such as the resource-based view and strategic alliances, which emphasize the importance of leveraging resources and forming partnerships to achieve strategic goals.

Needless to say, the above case studies take inspiration from Chapter 9, Verse 22 of the Bhagavad Gita, which highlights the importance of exclusive devotion, trust, and a selfless attitude towards partnerships.

By focusing on the needs of the partnership as a whole and being committed to its success, partners can achieve a greater level of success and fulfillment, just as devotees who worship with exclusive devotion are granted what they lack and have their needs preserved.

i. Continuous Improvement:

The Bhagavad Gita teaches the importance of continuous learning and self-improvement.

Chapter 4, Verse 38 of the Bhagavad Gita reads:

न हि ज्ञानेन सदृशं पवित्रमिह विद्यते ।

तत्स्वयं योगसंसिद्ध: कालेनात्मनि विन्दति ।। 4.38।।

na hi jñānena sadṛiśham pavitramiha vidyate
tatsvayam yogasansiddhaḥ kālenātmani vindati

"As a blazing fire turns firewood to ashes, O Arjuna, so does the fire of knowledge burn to ashes all reactions to material activities."

This verse can be interpreted as an encouragement to continually seek knowledge and self-improvement in order to overcome the limitations of our material desires and attachments.

Here Lord Shri Krishna encourages us to focus on knowledge and self-improvement in order to overcome the limitations of our material desires and attachments.

This is a powerful message for business leaders who seek to continually improve their organizations and themselves. By pursuing knowledge and self-improvement, business leaders can overcome the obstacles that prevent them from achieving their goals and create a culture of continuous improvement within their organizations.

The verse can also be interpreted as a call to action for business leaders to embrace change and innovation. Just as a blazing fire turns firewood to ashes, the fire of knowledge can burn away old ways of thinking and doing things.

This means that business leaders must be willing to challenge the status quo and continually seek new and better ways of doing things.

Furthermore, the verse emphasizes the importance of learning from our mistakes and failures. Just as fire burns away the impurities of firewood, the fire of knowledge can burn away the reactions to material activities, which can include our failures and mistakes.

⬦ ***Business leaders must be willing to embrace failure as an opportunity to learn and grow, and must encourage their employees to do the same.***

Overall, Chapter 4, Verse 38 of the Bhagavad Gita provides a powerful message for business leaders who seek to create a culture of continuous improvement within their organizations.

By focusing on knowledge, self-improvement, innovation, and learning from mistakes, business leaders can overcome the limitations of their material desires and attachments and achieve their goals.

i. Investment in talent :

The Bhagavad Gita emphasizes the importance of investing in oneself and developing one's skills and abilities. As Lord Krishna says in Chapter 2, Verse 7:

कार्पण्यदोषोपहतस्वभाव:

पृच्छामि त्वां धर्मसम्मूढचेता: |

यच्छ्रेय: स्यान्निश्चितं ब्रूहि तन्मे

शिष्यस्तेऽहं शाधि मां त्वां प्रपन्नम् || 2.7||

kārpaṇya-doṣhopahata-svabhāvaḥ
prichchhāmi tvāṁ dharma-sammūḍha-chetāḥ
yach-chhreyaḥ syānniśhchitaṁ brūhi tanme
śhiṣhyaste 'haṁ śhādhi māṁ tvāṁ prapannam

"You have a right to perform your prescribed duty, but you are not entitled to the fruits of action. Never consider yourself to be the cause of the results of your activities, nor be attached to inaction."

This verse emphasizes the importance of performing one's duty without being attached to the outcomes. In the context of management, this can be seen as investing in talent development for the long-term benefit of the organization, rather than focusing solely on short-term gains or individual rewards.

In modern management, there are several business theories that support the idea of investing in talent as a strategic approach to organizational success.

One such theory is the ***resource-based view*** of the firm, which suggests that a firm's competitive advantage comes from its unique resources and capabilities, including its human capital.

By investing in talent development, organizations can build a competitive advantage by creating a skilled and engaged workforce that can contribute to innovation and growth.

Another theory that supports investing in talent is the **human capital theory**, which posits that individuals' skills, knowledge, and experience are valuable assets that can lead to higher productivity, higher wages, and overall economic growth.

By investing in talent development, organizations can improve their employees' skills and knowledge, leading to higher productivity, better performance, and ultimately, higher profits.

Personal development theories also support the idea of investing in talent as a means of achieving long-term success.

For example, **Carol Dweck's growth mindset theory** suggests that individuals who believe they can develop their abilities through hard work and perseverance are more likely to achieve their goals.

By providing opportunities for employee development and growth, organizations can foster a growth mindset culture that encourages employees to take on new challenges and continually improve their skills and abilities.

One example of an organization that has successfully invested in talent development is ***Google.***

The company offers numerous employee development programs, including leadership training, mentorship programs, and technical skills training. These programs not only benefit the employees but also contribute to the company's success by fostering innovation and creativity.

To conclude, Chapter 2, Verse 7 of the Bhagavad Gita emphasizes the importance of investing in talent development for the long-term benefit of the organization.

This approach is supported by several business and personal development theories, and organizations that invest in talent development can build a competitive advantage, improve productivity and performance, and foster a culture of growth and innovation.

8. Impatience

I am very impatient person and my dad often chides me saying that, impatience causes more problems than stupidity.

He often highlights the fact that many problems arise from our inability to wait for things to naturally fall into place. This can lead to hasty decisions and actions that can create more problems than the ones we were originally trying to solve.

After I grew up, I found that Vedic philosophy echoed this very same in a verse from the Bhagavad Gita, which states:

sukha-duḥkhe same kṛitvā lābhālābhau jayājayau
tato yuddhāya yujyasva naivaṁ pāpam avāpsyasi

This verse (Chapter 2, Verse 38) emphasizes the importance of maintaining equanimity in the face of success and failure, gain and loss, and victory and defeat. It advises us to perform our duties with detachment, without being overly concerned with the results.

This is because our actions are ultimately within our control, but the results are not.

◇ An example of this can be seen in the corporate world, where impatience can often lead to rash decision-making.

For instance, a company might decide to launch a product prematurely, without properly testing it or gauging consumer demand. This can lead to negative consequences, such as poor sales or customer dissatisfaction.

On the other hand, if the company takes the time to conduct market research, gather feedback, and refine their product, they are more likely to succeed in the long run.

This idea of detachment and patience is also reflected in modern management theory, particularly in the concept of *agile methodology*.

Agile is an iterative approach to project management that emphasizes flexibility, adaptability, and collaboration. It encourages teams to break down complex projects into smaller, more manageable tasks, and to continually assess and adjust their approach based on feedback and data. This allows for greater responsiveness to changing circumstances and reduces the risk of making hasty, ill-informed decisions.

Another verse, where Lord Krishna emphasizes the importance of patience and equanimity in our actions is:

असंयतात्मना योगो दुष्प्राप इति मे मतिः |

वश्यात्मना तु यतता शक्योऽवाप्तुमुपायतः ||

|| Bhagavad Gita: Chapter 6, Verse 36 ||

asaṅyatātmanā yogo duṣhprāpa iti me matiḥ
vaśhyātmanā tu yatatā śhakyo 'vāptum upāyataḥ

This verse suggests that the mind can be restless and difficult to control, but with practice and detachment (vairagya), it can be brought under control. By cultivating a sense of detachment, we can learn to let go of the attachment to outcomes and focus on the present moment.

This verse is particularly relevant in the context of modern management theory, which emphasizes the importance of mindfulness and emotional intelligence in leadership.

◈ *Leaders who can remain calm and composed in the face of uncertainty and adversity are better equipped to make thoughtful, strategic decisions that benefit their organizations in the long term.*

For example, a leader who is faced with a crisis, such as a product recall or a financial setback, may be tempted to react impulsively and make decisions that are driven by fear or anxiety.

However, by cultivating mindfulness and detachment, the leader can step back and assess the situation objectively, gathering information and seeking input from others before taking action.

In addition, the practice of mindfulness and detachment can also help leaders to better manage their own emotions and responses to challenging situations.

This can lead to improved relationships with team members and stakeholders, as well as greater resilience and adaptability in the face of change.

One classic example, I always give of a leader who embodies the principles of mindfulness and detachment in their leadership style is : **Paul Polman,** the former *CEO* of **Unilever**.

Polman was known for his commitment to sustainable business practices and his ability to focus on the long-term goals of the company, rather than short-term gains.

Under Polman's leadership, Unilever pursued a "sustainable living plan" that aimed to reduce the company's environmental footprint while also increasing its social impact. This involved a focus on sustainable sourcing, reducing waste, and investing in community development projects.

Polman's leadership style was characterized by a sense of calm and equanimity, even in the face of challenges and setbacks. He was known for his ability to listen to diverse perspectives and to make decisions that were grounded in data and evidence, rather than emotion or personal biases.

For example, when faced with a hostile takeover bid from Kraft Heinz in 2017,

Polman resisted the pressure to make a hasty decision and instead focused on building a stronger case for Unilever's long-term value proposition.

He also emphasized the importance of treating all stakeholders with respect and care, including employees, customers, and suppliers.

Polman's approach to leadership is reflective of the principles of mindfulness and detachment espoused in Chapter 6, Verse 36 of the Bhagavad Gita. By cultivating a sense of detachment from short-term outcomes and focusing on the present moment, Polman was able to lead Unilever to greater success and impact in the long run.

So, here is a roadmap for cultivating mindfulness and detachment in leadership, based on the principles of Chapter 6, Verse 36 of the Bhagavad Gita:

    a) Start with self-awareness: Develop a deep understanding of your own emotions, thought patterns, and biases. This can involve practices such as mindfulness meditation, journaling, or seeking feedback from trusted colleagues.

b) Cultivate detachment: Practice letting go of attachment to outcomes and focusing on the present moment. This can involve techniques such as breath awareness, visualization, or reframing negative thoughts.

c) Build emotional intelligence: Develop the ability to recognize and manage your own emotions, as well as the emotions of others. This can involve practices such as active listening, empathy, and non-judgmental awareness.

d) Foster a culture of mindfulness: Encourage mindfulness and detachment in your team by modeling these behaviors and providing opportunities for reflection and self-awareness. This can involve practices such as group meditation, regular check-ins, and open communication.

e) Focus on the long-term: Prioritize long-term goals and values over short-term gains, and make decisions based on data and evidence rather than emotion or personal biases. This can involve practices such as strategic planning, stakeholder engagement, and measuring impact over time.

By following this roadmap, leaders can cultivate the principles of mindfulness and detachment in their leadership style, as exemplified by leaders like Paul Polman. This can lead to greater success and impact in the long run, as well as improved relationships with team members and stakeholders.

9. Conclusion

The Bhagavad Gita, one of the most influential Hindu scriptures, offers invaluable insights into the principles of entrepreneurship and leadership.

The timeless teachings of the Gita have been guiding people for centuries, and continue to offer practical wisdom to modern entrepreneurs and leaders.

Throughout this book, we have explored the key themes of the Gita, including the importance of self-awareness, the need for a strong sense of purpose, and the power of detachment.

We have seen how these concepts can be applied to the business world, helping entrepreneurs and leaders to navigate challenges and achieve success.

One of the key takeaways from the Gita is the importance of self-awareness.

The Gita emphasizes the need for individuals to understand their strengths and weaknesses, and to use this knowledge to make informed decisions. This is especially important for entrepreneurs and leaders, who must make decisions that can impact the lives of their employees, customers, and stakeholders.

Another important theme of the Gita is the need for a strong sense of purpose.

The Gita teaches us that we should act selflessly, without attachment to the outcomes of our actions. This approach can help entrepreneurs and leaders to focus on their mission and purpose, rather than being driven solely by the desire for profit or personal gain.

Finally, the Gita teaches us about the power of detachment.

This does not mean being indifferent or apathetic, but rather, it is about being able to detach oneself from negative emotions and distractions. This can help entrepreneurs and leaders to remain focused on their goals, and to make decisions that are not clouded by emotion or bias.

In conclusion, the Bhagavad Gita offers timeless wisdom that can help entrepreneurs and leaders to navigate the challenges of the modern business world.

By cultivating self-awareness, focusing on their purpose, and practicing detachment, entrepreneurs and leaders can lead their organizations to success while also fostering a sense of fulfillment and well-being for themselves and their teams.

As we continue to face unprecedented changes and uncertainties in the world of business, the teachings of the Gita are more relevant than ever, and can offer us guidance and inspiration as we strive to create a better future for ourselves and our communities.

As the author of this book,

I am grateful for the opportunity to share my insights on entrepreneurship and leadership through the lens of the Bhagavad Gita. I hope that this book has been a source of inspiration and practical wisdom for readers, and that it has provided valuable insights into the principles that can help individuals succeed as entrepreneurs and leaders.

I also welcome feedback from readers,

and

encourage you to share your thoughts and experiences with me.

If this book has been inspiring
and
there is a demand for further exploration of the knowledgebase on this topic,
I would be honored to write another book expanding on these ideas.
Thank you for taking the time to read this book,
and I hope that it has been a valuable addition to your personal and professional development.

————————————o——————————-

Acknowledgments

Alright, let's get real - writing a book is hard work,
and
I couldn't have done it without the support of some incredible
people.
Here's my chance to shout them out:
First and foremost, my family deserves a big shoutout.
They put up with my late nights, writer's block, and general
book-induced craziness.
Thanks for loving me anyway, guys.
Next up, a huge thank you to my mentors and coaches.
You've taught me everything I know about entrepreneurship and
helped me navigate the ups and downs of running a business.
I wouldn't be where I am today without your guidance.
I also have to give a shoutout to my fellow entrepreneurs, who
generously shared their stories and experiences with me. Your insights and advice have been invaluable in shaping this book and
making it relevant to real-life situations.
To the Vedic communities around the world - thank you for preserving and promoting the teachings of the Bhagavad Gita. Your
dedication to this ancient wisdom has made it accessible to people like me, who might not have discovered it otherwise.
And last but not least,

to all of you reading this - thank you for your interest and support.

I hope this book will inspire you to think differently about success and entrepreneurship, and maybe even make you laugh along the way.

Cheers to all my peeps!

Page intentionally left blank

Don't miss out!

Visit the website below and you can sign up to receive emails whenever ASISH DASH publishes a new book. There's no charge and no obligation.

https://books2read.com/r/B-A-EUJL-OUJIC

Connecting independent readers to independent writers.

Did you love *Entrepreneurship and Dharma : Gita Inspired Insights*? Then you should read *Insights From A Shy Entrepreneur*[1] by ASISH DASH!

[2]

Shy Entrepreneur Series : Volume -1

We have always been in awe of people who are successful and lead from the front.

However you will often find that, we individually have to make a continuous conscious effort in developing our skill set, by exploring resources available. There is no set course or book out there that can make you a complete leader. So much for the over-hyped and super-expensive MBA programs that just adver-

---

1. https://books2read.com/u/bzjAQz

2. https://books2read.com/u/bzjAQz

tise their placement numbers and salaries offered and don't really focus on skills.

This series of books will touch on some aspects that help you decode your weaknesses and give an alternative way of developing a mindset, a way of re-engineering your perception to problem solving to make you a more effective leader.It also uses the B.E.S.T. approach to leadership and certain other subtle processes that help you become a better leader and an entrepreneur.

Read more at https://in.linkedin.com/in/dashasish.

Also by ASISH DASH

The Shy Entrepreneur
Insights From A Shy Entrepreneur
Insights from a Shy Entrepreneur : Turning Slowdown into Opportunity

Standalone
Entrepreneurship and Dharma : Gita Inspired Insights

Watch for more at https://in.linkedin.com/in/dashasish.

About the Author

Asish Dash, is the Founder of Grazing Minds - the fastest growing sustainable consulting edtech platform.

Asish defines himself as 3E. (Engineer, Economist and Entrepreneur) an alumnus of world's Top 10 university and various other institutes.

Frugality in business, is his passion and so is creating low cost self sustaining business models.He loves talking, studying and decoding business models and innovation around it.

After 3 successful startups, He is all into sharing information. He believes writing books is one way in which he can connect to my audiences apart from the consulting he does on LinkedIn.

Though some of his opinions may be termed as brash and opinionated - but he says, he is not here to appease any corporations or lobbies!!

Read more at https://in.linkedin.com/in/dashasish.